This Notebook Belongs To :

Made in the USA
Middletown, DE
15 October 2023

40800268R00064